HISTORIC

COMMUNITIES

19th Century Clothing

Bobbie Kalman

Toronto · Oxford
New York

Crabtree Publishing Company

www.crabtreebooks.com

HISTORIC COMMUNITIES

Created by Bobbie Kalman

For Joan King

Editor-in-chief
Bobbie Kalman

Writing team
Bobbie Kalman
David Schimpky

Illustrations
Antoinette "Cookie" DeBiasi: cover, title page, pages 5, 8, 10, 18, 19, 22, 25. Colorized engravings: 11, 13, 20, 25, 26, 29
Barb Bedell: cover border, pages 6, 12, 14, 15, 23
Hilary Sandham: pages 16, 17, 21, 27

Research
David Schimpky

Editors
David Schimpky
N-Lynne Paterson

Separations and film
EC Graphics

Design and computer layout
Antoinette "Cookie" DeBiasi
Rose Campbell (cover mechanicals)

Printer
Worzalla Publishing

Art credits
The Albright-Knox Art Gallery, Buffalo, N.Y.
(*The Reception* by James Jacques Joseph Tissot): page 9
Courtesy of the Henry E. Huntington Library and Art Gallery, San Marino, California (*Girl holding a child by the hand* by Kate Greenaway): page 24

Photo credits
Bobbie Kalman: pages 5, 7 (bottom), 25, 26, 30 (both)
Ken Faris: pages 4 (bottom), 7 (top), 13
Black Creek Pioneer Village/TRCA: pages 4 (top), 28

Special thanks to
James Campbell
The students of Lakebreeze Elementary School

Published by
Crabtree Publishing Company

PMB 16A
350 Fifth Ave.,
Suite 3308
New York, N.Y.
10118

612 Welland Ave.,
St. Catharines
Ontario,
Canada
L2M 5V6

73 Lime Walk
Headington,
Oxford
OX3 7AD
United Kingdom

Cataloguing in Publication Data
Kalman, Bobbie, 1947-
   19th century clothing

(Historic communities series)
Includes index.
ISBN 0-86505-493-2 (library bound) ISBN 0-86505-513-0 (pbk.)
This book examines the clothes and accessories worn by 19th century men, women, and children in North America.

1. Costume - History - 19th century - Juvenile literature.
I. Title. II. Title: 19th century clothing. III. Series: Kalman, Bobbie, 1947- . Historic communities series.

GT620.K345 1993   j391'.00971

Contents

4   Pioneer clothing

6   Working clothes

8   Women's fashions

12   What men wore

15   Underwear

16   Footwear

18   Hats for every occasion

20   Cleanliness—a new idea

21   Hair styles

23   Sportswear

25   Children's clothes

29   Mass-produced fashions

30   Create a pioneer outfit

31   Glossary

32   Index

Pioneer clothing

The nineteenth century (1801 to 1900) was an exciting time of growth and prosperity in North America. Thousands of British, German, French, Swedish, Irish, Scottish, Italian, and Russian immigrants came from Europe to start new lives in the "land of opportunity." Many of these immigrants settled in wilderness areas. The people who made their homes in these rugged frontier lands were called **pioneers**.

The pioneers worked hard to build homes and feed themselves. There were no shops nearby where they could buy things. If they needed food, they had to hunt, fish, or gather it from the land. When their clothes wore out, they had to start from scratch to make new clothing.

*(top) The pioneers could not buy their clothes because they lived far away from towns and cities.
(above) Before wool and flax could be woven into cloth, they had to be spun into yarn on a spinning wheel.*

4

The clothing worn by the pioneers was made from simple, sturdy materials. The most available materials for making clothes were wool, flax, and leather.

The brake split the inner core of the flax plant.

Winter wool

To make wool, the thick winter coat of sheep was sheared off in the spring. It was washed clean of burrs and dirt, greased, fluffed up, and spun into yarn on a spinning wheel. The yarn was then dyed and woven into woolen fabric on a loom.

The fibers were combed on a hackle to get rid of the outer covering, leaving silky threads.

Flax to linen

The fibers of the flax plant were used to make **linen**, a lighter summer material. The seeds were removed, and the plant was soaked and dried. The inner core of the plant was broken on a gadget called a **brake**, and the fibers were combed on a **hackle**. The combed flax, called **line,** was spun into thread and then woven into linen. When wool and line were woven together, a new material called **linsey-woolsey** was made.

Clothing made of leather

Leather was often worn on the frontier because it was readily available. When animals such as deer or cows were killed for their meat, their skin or fur could be used to make clothing. Leather was made by **tanning** hides. To tan a hide, the skin was soaked in a chemical made from water and the bark of an oak or hemlock tree. It was then dried, greased, and softened by hand.

Buckskin, *which was leather made from deer hide, was used on the frontier to make jackets, boots, and pants.*

Working clothes

Many of the European immigrants who arrived in the early part of the nineteenth century became farmers. Since farmers worked outdoors, they needed tough, comfortable clothing. In summer these hard-working men wore loose-fitting linen or cotton shirts called **smocks**. Trousers were usually worn under the smock but, during very hot days, the smock was worn by itself. Large straw hats protected the farmers from the sun.

Pantaloons and overalls

In the middle of the nineteenth century, farmers began wearing high-waisted pantaloons that were held up by suspenders. A shorter white shirt, tucked into pants, replaced the smock. By the end of the century these pantaloons developed into overalls, which are still worn by many farmers today.

Clothes made from denim

In the west herds of cattle were tended by cowboys. Early cowboys wore denim coats, leather breeches, and tall boots. In later years cowboys also wore denim trousers or "jeans." In the 1850s a tailor named Levi Strauss began making and selling these denim trousers, which are now called "Levi's."

Cowboy hats

Cowboys wore huge hats that came to be known as "cowboy hats." They were classified in gallon sizes and were actually used for carrying water! Smaller hats were two-gallon hats, whereas the largest hats were called ten-gallon hats. These hats doubled as a wash basin or a bucket in which water was brought to a thirsty horse.

(top) The farmer on the left is wearing a smock over trousers. Later, farmers wore high-waisted trousers.
(below) Cowboys wore jeans, cowboy hats, and buckskin **chaps**. *Chaps protected the cowboy's pants and legs as he rode through thorny bushes.*

Rural women

During the week, women farmers wore simple dresses made of wool, linen, or linsey-woolsey. On Sundays they added a shawl or clean apron if they did not own a good dress. On their feet they wore thick, sturdy boots. Hats were a part of every outfit. Wide-brimmed straw hats or sun bonnets were necessary on sunny days. Indoors, women preferred mobcaps or cotton bonnets.

New fabrics for sale

As settlements grew, fabric was more easy to obtain. Frontier women were able to buy flannel and cotton from which they could make shirts, dresses, and simple suits for themselves and their family.

(top) The farmer above is wearing trousers held up by suspenders. (above) Rural women wore a cotton, wool, or linen dress protected by an apron. Mobcaps, bonnets, and straw hats were the most popular head coverings.

The leg-of-mutton sleeve was popular throughout the nineteenth century. It was given this name because it looked like a leg of lamb.

Hooped skirts were worn until the 1870s, when they were replaced by more closely fitting skirts.

Overcoats *were made of flannel, cotton, tweed, or water-repellent cloth. Many coats had cape collars that draped over the shoulder. The coat shown here has a double cape collar.*

Bodices were worn with skirts. They were snug at the waist.

Women's fashions

The basic outfit for nineteenth century women living in towns or cities was a combination of the hooped skirt, blouse, and **bodice**. Tight **corsets** and **bustles** gave women a thin-waisted look. Many dresses, blouses, and jackets had **leg-of-mutton** sleeves. The favorite materials for everyday wear were linen, wool, and cotton. Formal dresses, such as the one on the opposite page, were made from silk, velvet, satin, or lace.

The empire gown was worn in the early 1800s.

Flounced dresses were popular in the 1850s.

The princess gown was a one-piece dress that had buttons from the neck down to the floor. It was popular around the middle of the century.

(left) A woman named Amelia Bloomer introduced trousers to women. Although many people laughed at her, the outfit became famous, earning the nickname bloomers.

(right) In the 1870s the hooped skirts of the earlier days were replaced by tight ones that made walking difficult.

(far right) This casual suit was worn by women in the late nineteenth century. It was much more comfortable.

Empire gowns

In the early 1800s, women wore **empire gowns**. These high-waisted dresses were made of a nearly transparent fabric. A solid **petticoat** and a brassiere called a **zona** were worn underneath. The skirt descended straight to the ankle, and the sleeves could be short or long.

Middle-of-the-century dresses

During the 1850s lace dresses were very popular for formal occasions. They had tight bodices and long **flounced** skirts. The first suits for women consisted of a belted jacket worn over a hooped skirt. The **princess dress** was a popular gown in the 1860s. It was a floor-length, one-piece dress with a tight bodice and hooped skirt. The dress buttoned from top to bottom. Women also wore bloomers during this period.

Tight dresses

In the 1870s a new style of skirt became popular. It was floor length and full at the hips with a small bustle worn underneath. Walking was difficult in this skirt because it was tight around the knees! By the 1880s the bustle and skirt increased in size and bodices became longer. The "hourglass figure" came into fashion, and women wore tight corsets to make their waist look as thin as possible.

More practical clothing

Near the end of the century, women's clothes became more practical. Simple outfits such as a blouse and skirt were worn during the day. Some women also began wearing ties with their blouses. Suits consisting of a tight jacket and a loose skirt were popular as well, especially among women who worked in an office.

(below) A tight corset and large bustle created the "hourglass-figure" style that was popular in the 1880s. The long bodice is open to reveal the skirt, which matches the suit coat. The hat has a bird's nest on top and is typical of the decorated hats that were worn by women at that time.

1. The Beau Brummel look consisted of an unpatterned suit with a short waistcoat, a coat with tails, long, tight pantaloons, and a top hat.

2. The morning coat was short in the front and long at the back. 3. The norfolk jacket was a short belted sporty coat.

4. The frock coat was a long suit coat that looked like an overcoat.
5. The box coat resembled the suit jackets of today.
6. The Mackintosh was a long overcoat made of waterproofed material.

What men wore

An English gentleman named Beau Brummel changed the way men dressed in the early nineteenth century. He wore conservatively colored, fitted suits instead of the fancy, colorful ones of the eighteenth century. The most popular colors for this new style of suit were tan, green, brown, blue, gray, and black. The Beau Brummel look quickly spread across Europe and North America. Beau Brummel's influence can still be seen in the color of men's suits today.

Changing suit styles

Men's fashions did not change much throughout the nineteenth century. Suits composed of trousers, a waistcoat, and a coat were standard attire for men. Most of the fashion changes in men's suits were in the styling, or **cut**, of coats. Several different styles were popular. They could be single or double-breasted.

Long and short coats

The **frock coat** was a long, full coat with flared skirts. The **morning coat** was very popular for day or evening wear. It was short in front with long tails at the back. The **box coat** was short, had no waistline, and looked much like the suit coats of today.

Useful waistcoats

Although the **waistcoat** was called a "coat," it was actually more like a vest. It could be single or double-breasted and usually had two pockets in front for a gentleman's watch and **fob**.

Long pants instead of short ones

The biggest change in men's clothing from the eighteenth to the nineteenth century was the length of men's pants. **Breeches**, the knee-length pants of the eighteenth century, went out of style in the nineteenth century. Instead, men wore either **pantaloons** or **trousers**.

Pantaloons, which were also called **tights**, were popular among gentlemen. These pants were very tight and had a strap at the bottom that fit beneath the shoe or boot. Near the end of the century, creased trousers became fashionable in North America. To this day, men's pants have creases down the front and back.

(above) Everyday wear consisted of a shirt, waistcoat, and trousers. Suit coats were not always worn. (below) In cold weather, gentlemen wore overcoats, or greatcoats. The fancy fur-lined greatcoat shown below was worn on formal occasions.

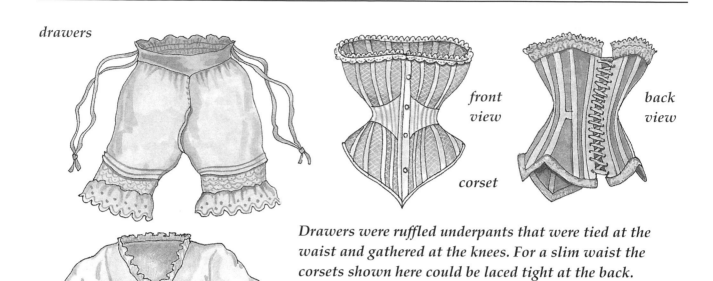

drawers

front view

back view

corset

Drawers were ruffled underpants that were tied at the waist and gathered at the knees. For a slim waist the corsets shown here could be laced tight at the back.

shift

Shifts *were worn next to the skin.*

Camisoles were loose and comfortable compared to corsets. They were worn at the end of the nineteenth century when women's fashions became more casual.

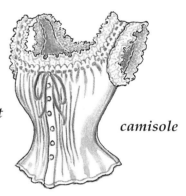

camisole

Crinolines gave skirts a full, hooped shape.
Bustles were worn under skirts to make them stand out at the back.
Petticoats fit under skirts. Some were plain; others had built-in bustles and layers of ruffles, such as the one shown below.

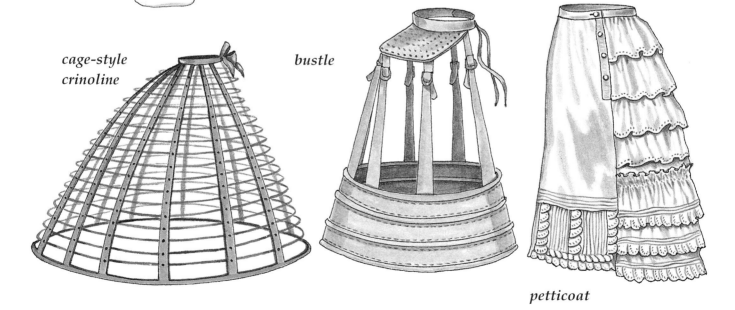

cage-style crinoline

bustle

petticoat

Underwear

Corsets, or **stays**, were an essential part of women's clothing in the nineteenth century. Some corsets fit a normal figure; others were laced tightly in order to give a woman a fashionably small waist. Near the end of the century, **camisoles** replaced the tight corsets.

Hoops and crinolines

Throughout most of the century fashionable skirts had a domed shape. Whalebone or metal hoops were sewn into petticoats to achieve this look. In the 1840s the **crinoline** was invented. At first the crinoline was a petticoat lined with horsehair and fitted with hoops to make a rigid dome. Later it developed into a light metal cage.

The bustle

By the 1870s the **bustle** replaced the crinoline in popularity. It made the back of a skirt much fuller, giving women a big-bottomed look. As the end of the century neared, skirts took on a more natural appearance and neither the bustle nor the crinoline were fashionable any longer.

Petticoats and drawers

Many people confuse **petticoats** and **drawers**. Petticoats were skirts of cotton, silk, or flannel that fit under regular skirts. Drawers were flesh-colored ruffled pants that were worn by women beneath their skirts. They became popular in the 1830s and have been worn by women in different forms ever since. Drawers were made of fine wool for winter and light cotton for summer. They were fastened with drawstrings around the waist and at the knees.

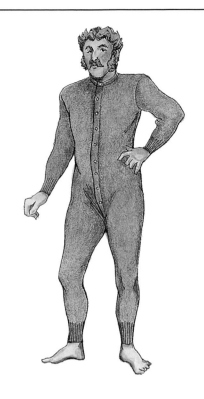

Most men wore cotton drawers and undershirts. Some wore a **union suit**. *This one-piece undergarment had a trap door at the back. Union suits came in red or white and kept men warm on cold winter days.*

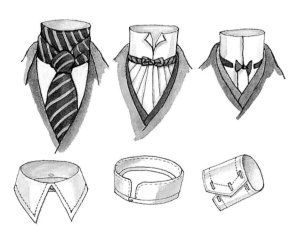

Cravats *and ties were worn with suits. Collars and cuffs were added separately to dress shirts.*

1. Roman sandals and 2. slippers were worn indoors. 3. Outdoor shoes extended above the ankle and were buttoned or laced. These shoes, called high shoes, had either a pointed or square toe.

4. On more formal occasions women wore silk or velvet shoes with small heels. These shoes were decorated with bows and usually matched the gown. Shoes with straps were also typical nineteenth century fancy footwear.

5. Canvas gaiters that buttoned up the side could be worn to protect shoes and stockings from the mud.

6. Pattens protected shoes by raising them above the ground.

Footwear

The people who lived in small villages or in the country usually wore leather footwear made by an **itinerant** shoemaker. This craftsman traveled the countryside and boarded with the families for whom he was making shoes and boots. The shoes were of plain leather, and the left and right shoes were identical. They were often several sizes too big so that more than one family member could wear them. Children also wore shoes that were too big so their feet could grow into them. For a better fit, the toes were stuffed with paper or cloth.

Stockings came in a variety of colors. The material from which they were made was called lisle. It was woven from fine cotton thread and was soft and durable.

Fancy women's shoes

Women living in large towns or cities wore **high shoes** outdoors. These shoes were fastened at the side with buttons or across the top with laces and could be made of soft black leather, **kid leather** (made from the hide of young goats), or kid and satin. At home or on formal occasions delicate slippers, called **pumps**, were worn. These were usually flat heeled and made of silk or kid. One version, called the **roman sandal**, was laced around the ankle like the sandals worn in ancient Rome. These delicate shoes were not suitable for walking outdoors.

Men's shoes and boots

Men wore boots in the winter and shoes in the summer. Footwear was almost always of soft black leather. Shoes had low heels, and laces replaced buckles, which were popular in the eighteenth century. Leather **oxfords** are one example of a late-century shoe style. The most common boots were called **Wellington boots**, named after the British Duke of Wellington.

Protection from mud

Both men and women wore **gaiters** to protect their stockings or pants from mud. Gaiters were canvas leggings that were strapped over the top of the shoe and buttoned up the side or front of the leg. **Clogs** or **pattens** were also used in bad weather. Clogs were thick soles that fit under shoes, whereas a patten was a metal ring that raised a shoe above the mud and kept it clean.

Shoes were often covered by gaiters.

The Wellington boot was worn until the 1870s.

*Rubber **galoshes** were invented near the middle of the century. They were ideal in muddy weather.*

Spatterdashes, **spats** *for short, became popular with formal black shoes.*

Both working men and women wore heavy leather shoes with thick soles.

laced high shoes

oxfords

The first tennis shoes (below) appeared in the 1880s. They had canvas uppers and rubber soles.

an early top hat
made of beaver felt

crown

brim

*Top hats were
worn throughout
the nineteenth
century. This
picture shows
a later style.*

*Straw hats were
ideal on sunny days.*

*The bowler hat, or derby,
was popular during the
middle of the century.*

*The homburg hat
was a later style.*

*a cap with
visor*

*The "deerstalker"
was a hunting hat.*

Hats for every occasion

During the nineteenth century both men and women wore hats every day. For the nineteenth century man the **top hat** was the most popular accessory. Top hats were made of silk or beaver felt and came in gray, tan, white, or black. Top hats had a tall crown and a narrow brim. A wide ribbon usually circled the base of the crown.

Derbies, straw hats, and homburgs

In the 1850s the **derby hat**, also known as the **bowler hat**, came into style. It was constructed of felt and had a rounded crown and a narrow brim. It was popular until the end of the century when the **homburg** came into style. The homburg was also a narrow-brimmed felt hat, but it had a dented crown. More casual headwear, such as straw hats with flat crowns and brims, was used in the summer. Caps with **visors** were worn for cycling and golfing. **Deerstalker hats** were hunting hats.

Women's hats

In the first part of the century, women wore **mobcaps**. These soft cloth caps became popular in the 1700s and were common until the 1860s. For the evening, elaborate turbans of silk, gauze, or velvet replaced mobcaps and bonnets.

The popular bonnet

Although women protected themselves from the sun by wearing straw hats decorated with ribbons or veils, by far the most popular hat of the century was the **bonnet**. This brimmed cap came in a variety of styles and was tied beneath the chin. It could be made of fur, velvet, satin, wool, straw, gauze, or cotton.

Soft linen caps were worn indoors.

cottage bonnet

drawn bonnet

poke bonnet

The **tall-crowned bonnet** was often decorated with ribbons and flowers.

The **sun bonnet** shielded the face from the sun's rays.

Mobcaps were worn at home.

Silky turbans were worn to fancy parties in the early 1800s.

Small hats were often decorated with birds' nests.

straw sailor hat

Straw hats came in many different styles.

Fancy hats

Smaller hats, which were more fashionable than practical, became popular in the 1860s. They were held on top of the head by a long hatpin and were decorated with feathers and ribbon. Straw sailor hats had a low crown and a brim that could be wide or narrow. They were also decorated with ribbon and flowers.

Large straw hats adorned with bows, feathers, and flowers were worn during the middle of the century.

(right) After the 1850s the "Saturday-night bath" replaced the once-a-year bath. Some children were not at all happy about this new trend.

(below) Long hair was popular during most of the century, although it was mainly worn up. Women were proud of their great manes. They only washed their hair about once a month, but women spent a great deal of time brushing it.

Cleanliness—a new idea

Ideas about cleanliness started changing during the nineteenth century. In the early 1800s Beau Brummel promoted good hygiene in England. He urged people to bathe daily and wash their clothes regularly. This seems like common sense to us but, in the nineteenth century, this thinking was quite new! In North America, cleanliness did not catch on until the 1850s. Before then people washed their clothes regularly, but they only bathed once or twice each year. They believed that the body's natural oils protected them from disease. By the end of the nineteenth century the "Saturday-night bath" was a tradition in many homes.

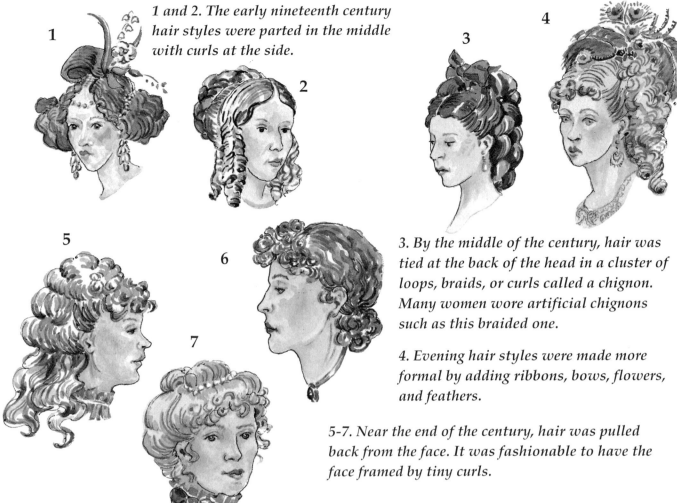

1 and 2. The early nineteenth century hair styles were parted in the middle with curls at the side.

3. By the middle of the century, hair was tied at the back of the head in a cluster of loops, braids, or curls called a chignon. Many women wore artificial chignons such as this braided one.

4. Evening hair styles were made more formal by adding ribbons, bows, flowers, and feathers.

5-7. Near the end of the century, hair was pulled back from the face. It was fashionable to have the face framed by tiny curls.

(below) 8. Before 1840 men's hair was worn long and wavy with a middle part. 9. For the rest of the century, hair was cut short. Facial hair also became popular. Men grew bushy side whiskers, mustaches, and beards.

Hair styles

The hair styles of the 1800s were very different from those of the 1700s. Wigs and huge hairdos were no longer in fashion. In the early part of the nineteenth century, women parted their hair in the middle. The hair over the ears was either pulled up on top of the head, or it hung down in curls. The hair at the back was also in ringlets or curls. Later on, **chignons** became popular. Chignons were ringlets, braids, or curls that hung at the neck or from the top of the head. By the end of the century, women wore their hair in much simpler styles—loose or tied in a plain bun.

Both men and women enjoyed the new pastime of going swimming or bathing. Bathing suits, especially women's, hid much of the body. Many women covered themselves with a large cape until they reached the water's edge.

(right) In the 1890s bicycle riding was a very popular sport. Men wore sports suits of flannel or linen with **knickers** and long stockings. Women wore bloomers such as the ones in this picture.

Sportswear

Both the men and women of the nineteenth century enjoyed sports of all kinds. Pastimes included hunting, riding, golfing, tennis, cycling, sailing, and bathing. Special sports clothes were developed for these activities.

What sporty women wore

For much of the nineteenth century little thought was given to sportswear for women. By the 1860s, however, women were involved in many sports, such as skating, riding, and hunting.

The attire for these activities did not differ much from ordinary clothes. It consisted of a jacket worn over a white shirt and long, full skirt. By the 1880s the skirts on sports clothes were shortened to above the ankle so that women could move more easily. Their feet and calves were covered by boots or shoes with gaiters.

The first bathing suits

In the 1860s doctors began promoting bathing in lakes and oceans as an aid to good health. The first bathing suits for women were made up of baggy trousers, over which a large, belted cotton shirt was worn. A net or bathing cap kept the hair in place. Men's bathing suits consisted of shorts and a short-sleeved shirt. (See bottom left picture on the opposite page.)

Men's sportswear

When taking part in sports, men wore a belted norfolk jacket and trousers or knickers. On their feet they had leather boots or shoes covered by gaiters. A soft cap with a visor or one with ear flaps kept the head warm.

The first professional baseball teams were formed in the 1870s. A uniform of knickers, a shirt, and a visored cap was developed for the sport. Baseball uniforms are much the same today.

The turtleneck sweater was a new addition to men's sportswear in the 1890s.

At the beginning of the nineteenth century, girls wore high-waisted empire dresses.

(above) Young girls wore short dresses. Ruffled trousers called pantalets covered their legs. (left) During winter, children enjoyed skating, tobogganing, and snowshoeing. The blanket coat was a popular cold-weather coat worn for these activities.

Everyday outfits for boys consisted of a cotton shirt, trousers, and suspenders.

Children's clothes

Young girls and boys wore cotton or linen smocks over **pantalets** until the age of four. After that age, girls and boys began to dress more like their parents. Boys were **breeched**, which meant they began to wear trousers. Girls wore dresses similar to those of their mothers.

Young girls wore fashionable adult-style dresses with crinolines. Their hairdos were also similar to those worn by their mothers.

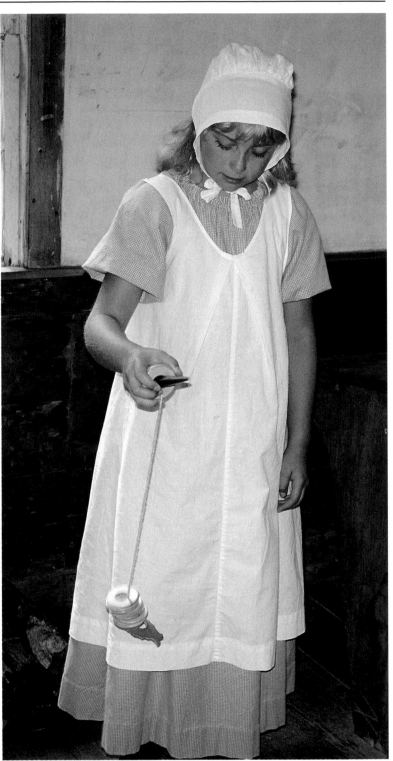

Knickers, stockings, a shirt, and jacket made up a boy's Sunday suit.

Many children only had two outfits—one for weekdays and one for going to church on Sundays. Everyday clothes for girls consisted of soft cotton dresses with a sash around the waist. Pinafores, such as the one worn by the girl above, covered dresses and kept them clean. If a girl only had one dress, she covered it with a clean pinafore or apron on Sundays.

Popular fashions for boys

Everyday clothes for boys were simple. A cotton shirt, trousers, and a cap or hat made up a basic outfit. During the 1850s and 1860s it became popular to dress boys in fancy clothes. **Sailor suits** with large collars were very popular, as were Scottish **kilts** and **tams**. The **zouave** suit had breeches and a short jacket decorated with braid. A shirt with a small collar was part of this outfit. These fancy fashions were worn throughout the rest of the century.

Just like their mothers

Girls dressed like their mothers, but the length of their skirts was shorter. One could easily tell the age of a girl by the length of her skirt! A girl of twelve had skirts that went just below the knee. For each additional year, the skirt was a little longer. At the age of eighteen young women wore full-length skirts. The hair styles of girls were also similar to those of women, including the addition of false curls.

Under and over

Girls wore a slip beneath their dress. After 1830 most girls also began wearing drawers. In the 1840s girls added crinolines to their under-clothing. They did not wear corsets until they turned eighteen.

Throughout the 1800s aprons or **pinafores** were used to protect girls' dresses. Aprons were tied around the waist. Pinafores hung from the shoulders and covered most of the dress.

Girls wore soft linen caps indoors and bonnets outdoors. During cold weather they wrapped themselves in a garment called a **wrapping cloak**. It was lined with fur, fleece, or wool.

Young boys were often seen in zouave suits (left) or sailor suits (right).

Near the end of the century, girls wore **reefer jackets,** *which had a large sailor collar.*

In the 1890s small children wore **brownie suits.** *These overalls, combined with the invention of cloth diapers and rubber pants, made it easy for small children to move and play. In earlier times small children had to play in bulky suits and dresses.*

Mass-produced fashions

The invention of new machines in the middle of the nineteenth century allowed clothing, shoes, and other items to be **mass-produced**, or made in large quantities. One of these inventions was the sewing machine.

As railroads were built to connect the cities of the east to the western parts of the country, ready-made clothing and thousands of other mass-produced items could be transported even to the smallest towns. This led to the founding of **mail-order companies** such as Sears-Roebuck and Montgomery Ward. Catalogs were sent to people all over the country, allowing them to order their clothes instead of make them. People who lived thousands of miles from each other were now able to wear the same fashions.

In the later part of the nineteenth century, people could buy almost anything they needed ready made. Some people shopped in large department stores (above), and others ordered their clothes from catalogs. On the right is a sample taken from a nineteenth century catalog. Notice the difference in the prices of clothes compared to the prices of clothing today. Even though these prices seem low to us, they were very expensive to nineteenth century shoppers. The salaries were much less in those days!

33934 Ladies' Spring Capes, 22 inches long, made of imported broadcloth, pleated ruffle collar of 1¾-inch ribbon, trimmed with black lace; black ribbon bow tie, shoulders and back trimmed with black braided scroll design producing a rich and handsome effect. Colors: Cardinal, red, navy blue, tan and black. Each........$5.00

33936 Ladies' Spring Capes, 22 inches long, made of ladies' broadcloth; collar made of fancy bows of satin ribbon; upper cape perforated in fancy designs. Colors: Black, tan, navy, cardinal; full sweep. Each....$5.00

33938 Ladies' Spring Capes, 21 inches long, turn-down collar; collar and skirt beautifully embroidered in two contrasting colors of silk braid. Full sweep. Colors: Tan, Havana, blue and black. Each.......$5.50

33940 Ladies' Spring Capes, 20 inches long, made of fine imported broadcloth. Turn down collar. Collar and bottom of skirt trimmed with narrow, fancy braid. 1½ inch fancy open-work lace two inches above bottom of skirt, fancy braided ornaments around shoulders and back. Colors: Navy, tan and black; full sweep. Each.......$5.50

33942 Ladies' Spring Capes, 32 inches long, made of imported black clay worsted, with 11-inch shoulder cape trimmed with jet and 8-inch ruffled collar. Satin ribbon bow in back and around neck. Each.........$6.00

33944 Ladies' Spring Capes, 22 inches long, double cape. B'lk broadcloth. Latest design, standing collar, with bow on side, 4 openwork designs in upper cape and two in lower cape with lace background. Colors: Black, red and navy blue. Each.................$6.00

Create a pioneer outfit

Have you ever wanted to dress like a pioneer? It is easy. You probably have most of the clothes right in your home! If you are a girl, you can wear a cotton dress or borrow a cotton skirt, an old-fashioned blouse, and an apron from your mother. A shawl or scarf can be worn over the shoulders. If you cannot get a bonnet, wear a straw hat decorated with flowers, birds, or fruit. Shoes with laces or straps are suitable footwear.

Boys can wear brown or black boots or laced shoes; woolen, cotton, or corduroy trousers with suspenders; and a country-styled cotton or flannel shirt. Hats can range from straw hats to caps with visors. Denim overalls are also suitable pioneer wear, as are knickers with long socks. Vests can double as waistcoats. Look through your closet or ask friends to lend you clothes that resemble the ones you see in this book.

(top) The children in this picture dressed pioneer style for an historic event. (above) These two girls experienced a week of pioneer living at a nineteenth century village.

Glossary

attire clothing, dress

Beau Brummel A fashionable English gentleman who influenced the color and style of men's clothing

bloomers Baggy women's trousers that were gathered at the ankle. They were named after Amelia Bloomer who started the fashion.

bodice The upper part of a dress or a fitted blouselike garment worn with a skirt

breeches Men's pants that extended just below the knees

buckskin Soft leather made from the skin of deer

bustle Padding or hoops that push out the back of a skirt

camisole A short-sleeved undershirt worn by women near the end of the nineteenth century

canvas A heavy, coarse material woven from cotton, hemp, or flax

chignon A roll of hair at the back of the head that is composed of braids or loops

craftsman A skilled worker, such as a tailor or carpenter, who makes items for sale

cravat A tie or scarf worn around the neck

crinoline A hooped petticoat

denim A strong cloth used for work clothes

department store A large store offering a wide variety of items for sale

double-breasted Describing a coat or waistcoat with two vertical rows of buttons down its front

drawers Short pants worn as underwear

eighteenth century The years 1701 to 1800

felt A fabric made from compressed wool or fur

flannel A soft cloth woven from wool or cotton

flax A plant used to make linen cloth

flounce A row of gathered or pleated material used to decorate women's dresses

fob An ornament attached to the end of a watch chain

frontier A region of new settlement

gaiters Leggings that cover the top of shoes and calves

galoshes Waterproofed overshoes

hygiene The practice of cleanliness and the prevention of disease

immigrant Someone who settles in a new country

itinerant Describing someone who travels from place to place

kilt A knee-length skirt, usually of plaid, that was originally worn by men in the Scottish Highlands

knickers Baggy breeches worn for sports

linsey-woolsey A material made by weaving wool and linen together

mail-order company A business that uses the postal service to deliver catalogs, receive orders, and send out ordered items

mass-produced Describing something made in large quantities. Factories allowed clothes, shoes, and other items to be mass produced.

nineteenth century The years 1801 to 1900

oxfords Low-cut leather shoes that laced up

petticoat A skirt worn beneath a dress

pinafore An apron worn by girls that hung from the shoulders and covered a dress

pioneer A person who settles in a new territory

salary The amount of money earned regularly by a worker

shawl A piece of cloth worn over the shoulders

shift A loose dress worn by women as underwear

smock A baggy shirt worn by farmers

spats A short cloth shoe covering worn with formal wear

stay A reinforced bodice that could be laced tightly. It was also called a corset.

suspenders A pair of straps worn over the shoulders to hold up a pair of pants

tam A round Scottish cap with a wool or feather bobble in the middle

turban A head covering made by winding cloth around the head

tweed A coarse woolen fabric used for suits and coats

visor The brim of a cap that extends out the front to protect the eyes from the sun

waistcoat A sleeveless buttoned jacket that was worn over a shirt and beneath a coat

whalebone The thin, strong material from the jaws of certain whales that was used for reinforcing corsets and crinolines

Index

apron 7, 26, 27, 30
baseball uniforms 23
bathing 20, 22, 23
bathing suits 22, 23
beards 21
Beau Brummel 12, 20
blanket coat 25
Bloomer, Amelia 10
bloomers 10, 11, 22
blouses 8, 11, 30
bodices 8, 11
bonnets 7, 18, 19, 27, 30
boots 5, 6, 7, 13, **16-17**, 23, 30
box coat 12, 13
brake 5
breeches 6, 13, 27
brownie suit 27
buckskin 5, 6
bustles 8, 11, 14, 15, 26
camisole 14, 15
cape collars 8, 12
capes 22
catalogs 29
chaps 6
children's clothing **24-27**
chignons 21
clogs 17
coats 6, 8, 11, 12, 13, 25
collars 8, 12, 15, 27
corsets 8, 11, 14, 15, 27
cotton 6, 7, 8, 15, 16, 18, 19, 23, 25, 27, 30
cowboy hats 6
cravats 15
crinolines 14, 15, 26, 27
cuffs 15
deerstalker hat 18
denim 6, 30
department stores 29
derby hat 18
drawers 14, 15, 27
dresses 7, 8, 9, 10, 11, 16, 24, 25, 26, 27, 30
empire gowns 10, 11, 24
farmers 6, 7
flannel 7, 8, 15, 22, 30
flax 4, 5
flounces 9, 10, 11
footwear (see shoes and boots)

frock coat 12, 13
frontier clothing **4-7**
fur 5, 13, 18, 27
gaiters 16, 17, 23
galoshes 17
greatcoat 13
hackle 5
hair 20, 21, 26, 27
hats 6, 7, 11, **18-19**, 30
high shoes 16, 17
homburg 18
hooped skirts 8, 10, 11, 14, 15
hourglass figure 11
hygiene 20
jackets 5, 8, 11, 12, 23, 26, 27
jeans 6
kid leather 17
kilts 27
knickers 22, 23, 26, 30
lace 8, 9, 10, 11
leather 5, 6, 16, 17
leg-of-mutton sleeve 8, 11
Levi's 6
linen 5, 6, 7, 8, 22, 25, 27
linsey-woolsey 5, 7
Mackintosh 12
mail-order companies 29
mass-produced fashions 29
men's fashion **12-13**
mobcaps 7, 18
Montgomery Ward catalog 29
morning coat 12, 13
mustaches 21
norfolk jacket 12, 23
overalls 6, 27, 30
overcoat 8, 12, 13
oxfords 17
pantaloons 6, 12, 13
pantalets 25
pattens 16, 17
petticoats 11, 14, 15
pinafores 26, 27
pioneers 4, 5, 30
pioneer clothes **4-7**, 30
princess dress 10, 11
railroads 29
ready-made clothing 29
reefer jacket 27
roman sandal 16, 17

ruffles 14, 15, 25
sailor hats 19
sailor suits 27
sandals 16, 17
satin 8, 9, 17, 18
Saturday-night bath 20
Sears-Roebuck catalog 29
sewing machine 28, 29
shawl 7, 30
shift 14
shirts 6, 7, 13, 23, 25, 26, 27, 30
shoemaker 16
shoes 13, **16-17**, 23, 29, 30
silk 8, 9, 15, 16, 17, 18, 19
skirts 8, 9, 10, 11, 14, 15, 23, 27, 30
slippers 16, 17
smocks 6, 25
spatterdashes 17
spinning 4
sportswear **22-23**
stockings 16, 17, 22, 26
straw hats 6, 7, 18, 19, 30
suits 7, 11, 12, 13, 22, 26, 27
suspenders 6, 7, 25, 30
tams 27
tanning leather 5
tennis shoes 17
tights 13
top hats 12, 18
trousers 6, 7, 10, 13, 23, 25, 30
turbans 18, 19
turtleneck sweater 23
underwear **14-15**
union suit 15
velvet 8, 16, 18
waistcoats 12, 13, 30
watches 13
weaving 4, 5, 16
Wellington boots 17
whalebone 15
whiskers 21
women's clothing **8-11**
wool 4, 5, 6, 7, 8, 15, 18, 30
working clothes **6-7**
zouave suit 27